MW01488439

JESUS

Son of Rahab

Restorative Devotional for the
Canceled and Disqualified

KERRICK
BUTLER II

Published by Harrison House Publishers
Shippensburg, PA 17257

ISBN 13 TP: 978-1-6675-0271-7
ISBN 13 eBook: 978-1-6675-0272-4

For Worldwide Distribution, Printed in the U.S.A.
1 2 3 4 5 6 7 8 / 26 25 24 23 22

Contents

INTRODUCTION

Have you ever felt like God could not use you because of your past? Perhaps you believe your past has disqualified you. Or maybe you wonder whether God has a plan for your life. Or if He did have a plan, you believe you destroyed your opportunity to fulfill it. As a result, you have limited yourself because of your own mistakes or the mistakes of your family line. If this struggle resonates with you, this devotional is for you.

Jesus Son of Rahab is for the cancelled, for those who think they have screwed up their lives, for those who feel robbed of a future because of the circumstances of their upbringing. We live in a world full of people who have limited themselves because they erroneously believe their past is more powerful than their future. As you read through this devotional, I want to help you overcome your past and step into the future God has for you.

The lineage of Jesus holds liberating truths, revealing God's ability and desire to use anyone who will dare to trust Him. This advent devotional will help you see your life in a fresh way, celebrate the Christmas season, and enter the new year with hope.

As we journey through advent together, I have provided scripture readings, reflection questions, faith confessions, and other assignments to help you implement these truths in your life. As you read this devotional, I urge you to complete the recommended reading and assignments and allow the truths contained in this book to radically impact your soul.

Your future is waiting. Let's start the journey together!

Day One

Beginning Our Journey Together

And because Joseph was a descendant of King David, he had to go to Bethlehem in Judea, David's ancient home. He traveled there from the village of Nazareth in Galilee. He took with him Mary, his fiancée, who was now obviously pregnant (Luke 2:4–5 NLT).

The Christmas season is upon us! People are hanging their decorations, ordering holiday-flavored drinks at coffee shops, streaming Christmas carol playlists on their smart phones, and rehearsing for Christmas cantatas. As we prepare for the season, have you ever considered that when we tell the real Christmas story, we often only focus on a small portion of the actual story?

Sure, we discuss Mary and Joseph, the magi, the shepherds, the angels, the villainous King Herod, and of course the birth of our wonderful Messiah. Yet, the Christmas story also includes the royal lineage of the Messiah, which is listed in Matthew 1. Not many sermons or carols focus on the lineage of Jesus at Christmastime. However, His lineage contains stories of scandalous relatives, individuals modern society would cancel, and the faithfulness of God.

When we think about all the people God could have chosen to be part of Jesus' ancestry, we probably think of the most righteous, most pious, and holiest individuals. But when we read the lineage, we discover a different story. God didn't just choose His superstars; He also chose people like Rahab. These people are relatable; they are a lot like us. They had issues and problems, challenges and shortcomings, just like we do. They made horrible decisions, like some of us have, yet God still included them in the ancestry of Jesus.

If God could use them as part of His plan to bring Jesus to the earth, God can definitely use us to fulfill His plan and purpose. God is an expert at taking messed-up lives and marvelously transforming them into miraculous lives. If you will let Him, God will do the same thing for you! Just as Mary and Joseph embarked on their journey to Bethlehem millennia ago, let's set out together on the journey into your future.

TODAY'S APPLICATION AND PRAYER

In a notebook or journal, honestly answer the following questions:

1. What would you like your future to look like?

2. What is the main problem from your past that is standing in the way between you and your future?

3. What makes you feel disqualified?

As you answer these questions, pray this prayer: "Father, help me to see the future You have for me. Help me to dream again, to dream bigger, and to clearly see the plan You have for my life. In Jesus' name, amen."

Today's Faith Confession

God has a plan for my life. He is marvelously transforming my life. Something good is going to happen to me today! I expect miracles!

Today's Scripture Reading:

Matthew 1

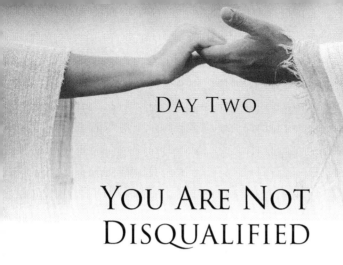

YOU ARE NOT DISQUALIFIED

For the gifts and the calling of God are irrevocable (**Romans 11:29 NASB**).

Reading through the lineage yesterday, did you notice some of the commentary provided by Matthew? I remember hearing a man of God jokingly say that if he was God, he would have edited some things out of the Bible—especially some of the disastrous decisions our heroes of faith made. Instead of removing the dirty laundry of the Bible, God left in the unedited stories, decisions, and consequences of the biblical characters for us to read and learn from.

After a holiday rush, the hottest new toy of the year is often gone from the shelves of every toy store, but plenty of other toys remain. Sometimes, stores put out discount bins holding toys with significantly reduced prices due to age or damage. Perhaps you have felt like one of those toys—discarded and useless after everything you have been through. But God did not leave you on the lonely shelf or place you in the shameful bargain bin.

The willingness God expressed in His dealings with Jesus' ancestors is the same willingness He has toward you. Your past has not disqualified you; the gift within you and the call upon your life are still real and relevant for today. As Romans 11:29 says, "The gifts and the calling of God are irrevocable" (NASB). God does not revoke your call when you screw up. He doesn't take His gift from you when you make a horrible mistake. He still has a plan for your life. You may have taken a wrong road in life, but today is the day you can get back on the path God has for you.

TODAY'S APPLICATION AND PRAYER

In a notebook or journal, honestly answer the following question:

1. What adjustment do you need to make to
   embark on the path toward your future?

As you answer this question, pray this prayer:
"Father, forgive me for the times I have missed it. Please
show me what adjustments I need to make so I can
embark on the path You have for my life. I receive Your
forgiveness and Your direction. In Jesus' name, amen."

Today's Faith Confession

God has a plan for my life. I choose to follow His
plan because His plan is far greater than mine. My past is
over. I am walking into my future.

Today's Scripture Reading:
1 John 1:9; Ephesians 2:10; Romans 8:1; Romans 10:29

Day Three

Whose Report
Will You Believe?

Mary responded, "I am the Lord's servant. May everything you have said about me come true." And then the angel left her (**Luke 1:38 NLT**).

When the angel Gabriel visited Mary to tell her she had been chosen to carry the Messiah, he also told her about her cousin Elizabeth's miraculous pregnancy. Mary later traveled to see Elizabeth, and when she arrived, Elizabeth's baby, John the Baptist, leapt within her womb, and she was filled with the Holy Spirit. At once, Elizabeth realized that Mary was carrying the Messiah, and she declared, "Blessed is she who believed, for there will be a fulfillment of those things which were told her from the Lord" (Luke 1:45).

Elizabeth called Mary blessed because she believed. Believe is the action word of faith. Faith is "firm belief, confidence, assurance, firm persuasion, the conviction of the truth of anything, belief with the predominate idea of trust." Mary believed what the angel told her, and Elizabeth prophetically declared what the result of her faith would be.

When we look at the lives of many of the individuals in Jesus' lineage, we discover that their faith separated them from the rest and enabled God to move greatly in their lives. A number of them are even listed in the Faith Hall of Fame found in Hebrews 11. Romans 10:17 tells us that "faith comes by hearing, and hearing by the word of God." These individuals heard what God said to them and about them. After they heard what He said, they had a decision to make. Would they believe Him? Or would they choose to reject His word?

As you read this devotional, faith will come to your heart and present you with a similar choice. Do you believe what God has said about you? You may say your life is too screwed up. Others may say you should be cancelled. Yet God says He has a plan for your life. Ask yourself the same question the prophet Isaiah asked millennia ago: "Whose report will you believe?" (see Isa. 53:1). I choose to believe the report of the Lord. I choose to believe what He says about me. Faith is a choice. You have to choose what you will believe. To enter the marvelous future God has for you, you must choose to believe what He says about you!

TODAY'S APPLICATION AND PRAYER

In a notebook or journal, honestly answer the following questions:

1. What do you believe about yourself?

2. Do any of your answers to the first question contradict what God's Word says about you?

As you answer these questions, pray this prayer: "Father, help me to see myself the way You see me. Help me to see myself according to what Your Word says. In Jesus' name, amen."

TODAY'S FAITH CONFESSION

I choose to believe the report of the Lord. I believe that God has a plan for my life. God is not finished with me. My best is yet to come!

TODAY'S SCRIPTURE READING:
Hebrews 11

Day Four

God Did Not Cancel You

If we confess our sins, He is faithful and just to forgive us our sins and to cleanse us from all unrighteousness (1 John 1:9).

At this time of year, millions of people are thinking about what gifts they want for Christmas, and many kids are making their Christmas lists. Some adults window shop and drop hints about what they would like to receive. Others may create a wish list on an online retailer and share it with others. In the Christmas carol, "The Twelve Days of Christmas," the main character of the song receives a total of 364 gifts. Gifts are a big deal to us, and they are a big deal to God too.

God is a gift-giving God. He delights in giving good gifts. Jesus even said that the Father experiences great happiness in giving us the Kingdom (see Luke 12:32 NLT). Gifts are not something we can earn, but something we receive—like forgiveness.

Forgiveness is a gift. People truly want to be forgiven. But when we look at the regrets in the past, we know we cannot do anything to earn forgiveness for our sins. We cannot work hard enough or do enough good deeds to cancel our sins. However, we can receive forgiveness, which completely obliterates all of our sins. If you have asked God to forgive you, He has truly forgiven you. You have to accept that fact by faith. Forgiveness is not a feeling, but a gift from God that you receive. When you feel guilty about your past, remind yourself that you have been forgiven.

At its root, forgiveness is a financial term. It is the cancellation of a debt. Imagine a man who owes hundreds of thousands of dollars. He wants to pay off the debt, but it seems insurmountable. One day, the creditor calls to inform the man that he no longer owes anything. The debt has now been cancelled. Would that man feel guilty that he no longer owed a huge debt? No!

He would feel relieved, joyful, and grateful. He might even be inspired to show generosity to others.

When you asked God to forgive you, He actually forgave you. It's time for you to believe that God did exactly what He said. He has forgiven you from all your sins and cleansed you from all unrighteousness. Others may try to cancel you, but I have news for you: God did not cancel you. He cancelled your debt of sin. Now, you are forgiven.

TODAY'S APPLICATION AND PRAYER

In a notebook or journal, honestly answer the following questions:

1. Are you trying to do anything to earn forgiveness? What you are doing may be a good thing, but if the motive is to earn forgiveness from God, you'll end up frustrated and disappointed.

2. Is there anything you haven't forgiven yourself for? Sometimes people have a hard time believing God has forgiven them because they have a hard forgiving themselves. God has forgiven you. You need to forgive yourself.

As you answer these questions, pray this prayer: "Father, thank You for forgiving me. Help me to see forgiveness as a gift and not something I earn. Help me to forgive myself and move into the future You have for me. In Jesus' name, amen."

TODAY'S FAITH CONFESSION

God did exactly what He said He would do. He has forgiven me of all my sins, and He has cleansed me from all unrighteousness. I am not cancelled; my debt is cancelled. I have been forgiven by God, and I forgive myself.

TODAY'S SCRIPTURE READING:

Luke 7:36–50; Matthew 9:2; 1 John 2:1–2

Day Five

God Loves Giving You Gifts

Every good gift and every perfect gift is from above, and comes down from the Father of lights, with whom there is no variation or shadow of turning (James 1:17).

Gift giving is a hallmark of the Christmas season. People purchase gifts for family, friends, loved ones, co-workers, secret Santa exchanges, and more. Over the next week and a half, stores will be full of shoppers, and e-commerce sites will orchestrate mass deliveries all over the world. We love to give gifts because we are like our heavenly Father, who is a gift-giving God. He delights in giving gifts. The original language of James 1:17 implies that God is in the habit of giving good gifts. The phrase *comes down* paints the imagery of a thunder shower. In other words, God habitually rains good gifts on His children just like water pours from the sky during a rainstorm.

Some kids think they can be sneaky and open their Christmas gifts early. Perhaps you were one of them. The good news is, God has a gift for you that He wants you to open and enjoy immediately—the gift of righteousness. Romans 5:17 says we receive, through Christ, "abundance of grace and of the gift of righteousness," which enables us to "reign in life." The next verse clarifies that this is a "free gift" given to all people, "resulting in justification of life" (Rom. 5:18). In addition, 2 Corinthians 5:21 declares, "For He made Him [Jesus] who knew no sin to be sin for us, that we might become the righteousness of God in Him."

God gives the gift of righteousness to all who put their faith in Jesus. God's gift of righteousness is a change of status in which you are made the righteousness of God in Christ Jesus. Righteousness is your standing; it is also your identity. Since righteousness is your standing, you can go before the throne of God and receive grace, mercy, and help in your time of need (see Heb. 4:16).

When you identify as the righteousness of God in Christ Jesus, you no longer identify with your sin. When you were a sinner, you did good things, but those good things did not make you righteous. Now that you are righteous, when you sin, it doesn't reverse your status. You became righteous because of your faith in Jesus, not because of the good things you did.

To successfully enter your future, you must see yourself as righteous. If you identify with your past, seeing yourself as a sinner, you will not fully experience the future God has for you. You are no longer a sinner; you have been saved by grace. Now you are the righteousness of God in Christ Jesus.

TODAY'S APPLICATION AND PRAYER

In a notebook or journal, honestly answer the following questions:

1. Are you identifying with any negative areas of your past (a sin, addiction, trauma, or bad habit)?

2. How will you apply the truth that you are the righteousness of God in Christ Jesus

to what you have previously identified with?

As you answer these questions, pray this prayer: "Father, thank You for the gift of righteousness. Help me to see myself as righteous and not as a sinner. Help me to renew my mind in this area so that I can experience what You have for me. In Jesus' name, amen."

TODAY'S FAITH CONFESSION

I am not an old sinner, saved by grace. I have been saved by grace. I am now the righteousness of God in Christ Jesus. I am who God says I am, and I choose to see myself that way. Because God has made me righteous, I can go into my future and experience the best of what God has for me.

TODAY'S SCRIPTURE READING:

Romans 5

Day Six

Tidings of Comfort and Joy

Glory to God in the highest, and on earth peace, goodwill toward men (Luke 2:14).

Because the heavenly host made this exclamation of praise on the night that Jesus was born, peace and goodwill are often associated with this marvelous season. Greeting cards proclaim "Peace on Earth," and Christmas songs sing about peace throughout the world. But what did the angels mean? They were declaring God's decision (in the birth of Jesus) to send peace and goodwill to humanity.

In Acts 10:36, the apostle Peter explained that God offers us peace with Him through Jesus Christ. This is what the angels were celebrating, and we need to join in the celebration. God is not out to get us. He loves us and has goodwill toward us. Whether you recently made a decision to follow Jesus, have just recommitted your life to Him, or have been following Him for a long time—God is not mad at you. Through Jesus Christ, we find peace with God. Not only that, but God's plans for our lives are good. His plans are part of His goodwill toward us. These are "the tidings of comfort and joy," the good news we are called to "tell on the mountain."

As you progress through this devotional, remember that God has given you the gifts of forgiveness and righteousness. Never forget that because of Jesus you have peace with God and His plans for your life are good. In similar fashion to the old heralds who would cry in the town square and announce the new day and the news of the day, I've written this devotional to declare your new day. You get a fresh start!

The first six days of this devotional are designed to help you understand what God has already done for you and His desire for you to experience the future He has for you. Over the next two weeks, we'll look at different individuals in Jesus' lineage. As we examine His lineage, we'll discover lessons that will help you move into your divinely designed future. Your new day has begun. Your best is yet to come. Your future will be greater than your past.

TODAY'S APPLICATION AND PRAYER

In a notebook or journal, honestly answer the following questions:

1. What does it mean to you to be given a fresh start?

2. How does the truth that you have peace with God impact the way you view your relationship with God?

As you answer these questions, pray this prayer: "Father, thank You for the gifts of forgiveness and righteousness. I am so grateful that I have peace with You. Help me to make the most of the fresh start You have given me. Over the next two weeks, please give me insight into how to move into my future as I study the lineage of my Savior. In Jesus' name, amen."

TODAY'S FAITH CONFESSION

I have peace with God through Jesus Christ. I am not estranged from God. I have been brought close to

Him through Jesus. I have received the gifts of forgiveness and righteousness. God's plans for my life are good. He has goodwill toward me.

TODAY'S SCRIPTURE READING:
Ephesians 2

THE SON OF ABRAHAM

This is a record of the ancestors of Jesus the Messiah, a descendant of David and of Abraham: Abraham was the father of Isaac. Isaac was the father of Jacob. Jacob was the father of Judah and his brothers (**Matthew 1:1–2 NLT**).

Have you ever watched a Christmas special narrated by a kind, elderly gentleman? The Christmas story of our salvation has a grandfather figure as well—Abraham. He is one of the most important characters in the Christmas story, although he is rarely mentioned.

It's true that Abraham is not part of the traditional Christmas story, and he was not in the stable or fields the night Jesus was born. Yet, as an ancestor of Jesus, he played a crucial role. Abraham's faith opened the door for the Messiah to be born into the world. When God appeared to Abraham in Ur, God declared that through Abraham all nations would be blessed (see Gen. 12:1–3). When God promised Abraham an heir, Abraham "believed the Lord, and the Lord counted him as righteous because of his faith" (Gen. 15:6 NLT). God counted Abraham, a moon worshipper from modern-day Iraq, as righteous because of what he believed. His past as a moon worshipper did not prevent his righteousness. His mistakes could not discount his righteousness. He believed what God said, and as a result, He was counted righteous.

In Abraham's faith journey, he made many mistakes and learned many lessons. Before his faith matured to the point that it opened the door for the Messiah to be born, he had to leave his past behind. He had to leave Ur. He had to leave Haran. He had to leave those places so he could enter into the future God had for him. Abraham's faith led him to leave the comfort zones of his past. The same will be true for you.

Unless you set out on a faith journey, like Abraham did, it will be easy to return to your old ways of life even though you know they are not God's best for you. Your faith journey begins with a quality decision to leave your past behind. A quality decision is a decision that is reinforced by supporting decisions every moment, hour, and day afterward. Your past is not worth returning to; the future God has for you is brighter than you can imagine.

To walk into your future with faith like Abraham, you must believe the promise God has made to you—God is not finished with you, and He has a plan for your life. My cousin, Pastor Andre Butler of Faith Xperience Church in Detroit, likes to say it this way: "With faith, there is a future."

TODAY'S APPLICATION AND PRAYER

In a notebook or journal, honestly answer the following question:

1. What are some quality decisions that you need to make?

As you answer this question, pray this prayer: "Father, thank You for the future You have for me. Reveal to me the quality decisions that I need to make. Please strengthen me to make those decisions and not back away from them. I gratefully receive Your help and Your strength. In Jesus' name, amen."

TODAY'S FAITH CONFESSION

My past is not worth returning to. God has a bright future for me. I choose to leave my past behind and enter into the future God has for me. Today, my future begins.

TODAY'S SCRIPTURE READING:

Genesis 12

DAY EIGHT

THE LANGUAGE OF YOUR FUTURE

The Lord had said to Abram, "Leave your native country, your relatives, and your father's family, and go to the land that I will show you. I will make you into a great nation. I will bless you and make you famous, and you will be a blessing to others. I will bless those who bless you and curse those who treat you with contempt. All the families on earth will be blessed through you" (**Genesis 12:1–3 NLT**).

In Charles Dickens' tale, *A Christmas Carol,* Ebenezer Scrooge is visited by the ghosts of Christmas past, present, and future. These apparitions invite Ebenezer

31

Scrooge to change his ways and change his future. While I'm not going to appear in your room and take you through your life journey dressed in an elaborate costume (as in the novel), I do want you to start your day knowing that God has a wonderful future for you.

As we saw yesterday, Abraham had to leave his past to access his future. Abraham's original name was Abram, but on his faith journey with God, God changed his name and his wife's name. He did this to change the way Abraham talked. For years, Abram and Sarai had not been able to have children. I'm sure this experience influenced the way they talked. So God changed their names. Abraham means, "father of many nations." So after his name change, every time Abraham introduced himself, he identified with his future. Every time Sarah called his name, she spoke over him that he was the father of many nations.

In the same way, it is time for you to identify with your future. What are you saying about yourself? You are not who you used to be. You left your past behind. If you continue to talk the way you did before or you verbally identify with your past, you will return to your past. The words of your mouth must match the quality decision you made yesterday. One of the reasons I provide confessions throughout this devotional is to help you change the way you speak. Your words have the power to limit you—or to propel you. The wrong words can keep you from entering your future.

You don't need to change your name, but you do need to change the way you talk about yourself. You are not stupid. You are not worthless. You are not a mistake. You are not a failure. You are not hopeless. Your life is not over. God has a wonderfully bright future for you; it's time you talked like it!

Today's Application and Prayer

In a notebook or journal, honestly answer the following questions:

1. What are some negative things that you need to stop saying?

2. What are some positive things, based on God's Word, that you can say about yourself?

As you answer these questions, pray this prayer: "Father, thank You for Your Word! Help me to talk about myself in a way that aligns with your Word. Help me to refrain from speaking negatively about myself. Help me not to limit my life with the words of my mouth. Help me to say what You say about me. In Jesus' name, amen."

TODAY'S FAITH CONFESSION

I am who God says I am. God's promises will come to pass in my life. My past is not strong enough to cancel my future. I am a child of the Most High God. I am not a failure. I am not a mistake. I am not stupid. I am not worthless. I am not hopeless. I identify with the promises of God. My life is not over; my best days are just getting started.

TODAY'S SCRIPTURE READING:
Genesis 17

DAY NINE

A CHRISTMAS MIRACLE

Give thanks to him who alone does mighty miracles. His faithful love endures forever (**Psalm 136:4 NLT**).

Christmas movies are streaming on channels everywhere right now. The arc of many of these Christmas stories involves people who need a "Christmas miracle." In these arcs, hope seems lost, but all of a sudden, an unforeseen "miracle" positively turns the hopeless situation around. If anyone in biblical history needed a "Christmas miracle," it was Abraham and Sarah. For decades, they had been trying to have a child, but without success.

Perhaps you can relate. You have tried to live differently, to birth something new in your life, but without any success. Now, you believe your situation is hopeless because of the epic mistakes you've made. Or maybe it feels hopeless because no one in your family has ever escaped the situation you were born into. If you feel like you need a Christmas miracle, I'm here to give you the good news—your Christmas miracle is the game plan of Abraham.

Yesterday, we saw that God changed how Abraham talked about himself. That was step one of the game plan. Step two was simple: Abraham believed in hope even though it looked hopeless (see Rom. 4). What has God said about your future that seems like a dream that is out of your reach? If you dare to believe that it will come to pass, just like Abraham did, that divine dream will be your reality. Romans 4 says Abraham was not weak in faith; in other words, he did not consider the contradictions to the promise. God had promised Abraham and Sarah that they would have a son. The problem was that Abraham was 99 and Sarah was 90. But Abraham "did not consider his own body, already dead (since he was about a hundred years old), and the deadness of Sarah's womb" (Rom. 4:19).

If you always think about all the reasons why what God says about your future cannot come to pass, then you will be weak in faith. When you think about the future, what contradictory reasons keep popping up in your head? What excuses are keeping you from your future? Those reasons and excuses are contradictions to faith, screaming at you, "It won't happen!" If you listen to them, God's promises probably won't happen for you. But if, instead, you make the Abrahamic decision to ignore the contradictions, you will be one step closer to the future God has for you.

TODAY'S APPLICATION AND PRAYER

On a piece of paper, write down all of the excuses and reasons why you think you cannot enter the wonderful future God has for you.

Afterward, pray this prayer: *"Father, thank You for helping me define myself according to Your Word. Please help me to follow the example of Abraham's faith. Help me to believe and choose hope. In Jesus' name, amen."*

TODAY'S CONFESSION

Point at the paper on which you wrote down all the false excuses and reasons, and declare: These things do not define me. I refuse to allow these contradictions to limit me. I am following the example of Abraham. What God promised will come to pass in my life!

Now throw that piece of paper away.

TODAY'S SCRIPTURE READING:
Romans 4

DAY TEN

GLORY TO GOD IN THE HIGHEST

Give thanks to the LORD, for he is good! His faithful love endures forever (**Psalm 136:1 NLT**).

One of my favorite things about this season is the music—both recorded carols and live performances. How soon is too soon to start listening to Christmas music? I enjoy playfully debating with my siblings and friends about the appropriate time to play my first Christmas carol of the season. All of the musical sounds of the season remind me of the heavenly host of Luke 2. To the great surprise of the shepherds, the heavenly host filled the field with praises to God, proclaiming, "Glory to God in the highest!"

Although we may disagree on when is the best time to begin playing Christmas music, we can agree that it is never too early give glory to God just like Abraham did centuries before the angelic celebration of the Messiah's birth. Abraham did not waver in his faith concerning God's promise, but instead, he stayed strong in faith and gave glory to God (see Rom. 4:20). Strong faith gives glory to God before the miracle happens. After refusing to consider his circumstances, Abraham changed the way he talked, and he consistently praised God that His promise was coming to pass.

Praise is the pathway to a miraculous transformation. As we talked about previously, to step into our future, we must change the way we think and talk about ourselves. Next, we need to praise God in faith that what He has said about us is true.

One simple way to do this is to say, "Father, thank You for forgiving me. Thank You for washing away my sin. Thank You for redeeming me. Thank You for transforming me into a new creation in Christ Jesus." Simply thanking God for what He has done will help you move forward into your future. In addition, look for songs that remind you of the work God has already done and songs that declare the future God has for you. If you listen to these songs consistently and continuously sing praises to God, you will follow in Abraham's steps and strengthen your faith.

TODAY'S APPLICATION AND PRAYER

In a notebook or journal, honestly answer the following questions:

1. Are there any songs that you need to stop listening to?

2. What is a song that reminds you of the future God has for you?

As you answer these questions, pray this prayer of thanksgiving: *"Father, thank You for forgiving me and washing away all of my sin. Thank You for being my redeemer. Thank You for being my healer. Thank You for being my provider. Thank You for being my savior. Father, I thank You for the wonderful future You have prepared for me. I give You all the glory, honor, and praise for what You have done in my life and for what You will do in my life. I join in with the angels of old and say glory to God in the highest. In Jesus' name, amen."*

TODAY'S FAITH CONFESSION

I am who God says I am. I believe what God says about my future. As a result, I choose to glorify God. I choose to be joyful. I choose to be grateful. My best is yet to come, and I am thankful!

TODAY'S SCRIPTURE READING:

Psalm 100

DAY ELEVEN

HOLIDAY ROAD TRIPS

The next morning Abraham got up early. He saddled his donkey and took two of his servants with him, along with his son, Isaac. Then he chopped wood for a fire for a burnt offering and set out for the place God had told him about (**Genesis 22:3 NLT**).

Have you ever traveled over the holidays? Whether by car or plane, holiday travel can often be hectic and stressful because so many other people are also traveling—and because one must remember everything needed for the trip. It reminds me of the less-then-ideal "road trip" that Abraham and Isaac took. God told Abraham to take his son Isaac—the promised son—to Moriah and offer him as a sacrifice (see Gen. 22:1).

Abraham did as God said, saddling his donkey, splitting the wood for the sacrifice, and bringing along Isaac and two servants. After three days of travel, they arrived at the place, and Abraham and Isaac went ahead alone. As they walked together, Isaac asked his father where the lamb for the sacrifice was. Abraham said, "My son, God will provide for Himself the lamb for a burnt offering" (Gen. 22:8).

This event in Genesis 22 opened the door for the true meaning of Christmas and the wonderful future God has for each of us. Let me explain. In God's covenant with Abraham, each party had to be willing to do what the other party was willing to do. In Genesis 22, God put that to the test. If Abraham was willing to offer his son, then God could legally offer His Son for the sins of humanity. Abraham understood his covenant and set out on this road trip with Isaac to fulfill his part of the covenant.

Hebrews 11 tells us that Abraham undertook this journey in faith, even believing that God was able to raise Isaac from the dead if it came to it. We see Abraham's faith through what he said on the trip to the mountain. First, Abraham told his servants that both he and Isaac would return (see Gen. 22:5). Second, Abraham told

Isaac that God would provide a lamb (see Gen. 22:8). When it came time for the sacrifice, God provided a ram in the bush as a substitute for Isaac. The prophesied Lamb is introduced in John 1:29, where John the Baptist declared about Jesus, "Behold! The Lamb of God who takes away the sin of the world!"

God provided a Lamb! He sent Jesus, the Lamb of God, to take away our sins. The Lamb has overcome every sin and shortcoming you think disqualifies you from a wonderful future. When you ask God to forgive you, He actually does, because Jesus paid the price for your sins.

TODAY'S APPLICATION AND PRAYER

In a notebook or journal, honestly answer the following question:

1. What is the first thing that comes to mind when you realize the Lamb of God has carried away all of the disqualifications of your past?

As you answer these questions, pray this prayer: "Father, thank You for providing a Lamb for us and forgiving all my sins. Thank You for giving me a brand-new life. In Jesus' name, amen."

TODAY'S FAITH CONFESSION:

God has forgiven me all of my sins. I have a Savior. He is the Lamb of God, and because of His blood, I can live free of sin, condemnation, guilt, and the consequences of sin. My future is bright because of the blood of the Lamb of God, which He shed for me.

TODAY'S SCRIPTURE READING:

Genesis 22

HE MADE YOU WORTHY

Then I looked again, and I heard the voices of thousands and millions of angels around the throne and of the living beings and the elders. And they sang in a mighty chorus: "Worthy is the Lamb who was slaughtered—to receive power and riches and wisdom and strength and honor and glory and blessing."

And then I heard every creature in heaven and on earth and under the earth and in the sea. They sang: "Blessing and honor and glory and power belong to the one sitting on the throne and to the Lamb forever and ever."

And the four living beings said, "Amen!" And the twenty-four elders fell down and worshiped the Lamb (Revelation 5:11–14 NLT).

"Worthy is the Lamb" echoes throughout the heavenly throne room. Here we see the inhabitants of heaven declaring Jesus' worthiness because of the sacrifice He made to cleanse us from sin and redeem us back to God.

The Lamb's sacrifice was so effective that it made us worthy. We are no longer unworthy. The blood of the Lamb washed away our sins, faults, and shortcomings. God's love for us—and the wonderful future He has for us—is not based on what we have done. It is based on what Jesus has done. God is not the keeper of a "Naughty or Nice List."

When you decided to make Jesus your Lord, you positioned yourself to receive all of the wonderful gifts God has for you. Imagine a Christmas morning filled with a loving family and cherished friends. As children come down the stairs in the morning, they find a tree surrounded with wrapped gifts of all sizes. After the children take their places around the tree, the mother hands gifts to each child. How would the children respond—gleeful ripping of wrapping paper, wide smiles on faces, shouts of gratitude? All of these classic reactions to gifts on Christmas morning seem logical to us.

But what if, unexpectedly, a child refused to receive the gift? Instead, he or she says, "Please take the gift back. I am unworthy to receive this gift." As shocking as that would be, sadly many Christians treat God's gifts the same way. God's forgiveness and the future He has for you are gifts. You do not earn a gift. You do not have to get on God's "nice list" to receive it. You are already there because of Jesus. When He hands you a gift, all you have to do is receive it. The future God has for you is part of His gift of grace to you, which you must receive by faith (see Eph. 2:8).

Stop saying you are unworthy of God's gift. The blood of Jesus made you worthy; the Lamb of God has done everything necessary for you to receive the wonderful gifts God has for you.

TODAY'S APPLICATION AND PRAYER

In a notebook or journal, honestly answer the following questions:

1. What makes you feel unworthy?

2. What has feeling unworthy kept you from experiencing?

3. How will you combat giving into feelings of unworthiness?

As you answer these questions, pray this prayer: "Father, thank You for providing a Lamb for us. Thank You for washing away my sins. Thank You for making me worthy through the blood of Jesus. Help me to stop giving in to feelings of unworthiness. Help me to realize all that the blood of Jesus has done for me. I join in with heaven and declare, 'Worthy is the Lamb of God!' Thank You for providing Your Lamb for me. In Jesus' name, amen."

TODAY'S FAITH CONFESSION

God has forgiven me. The blood has made me worthy to enter into the future God has for me. I refuse to disqualify myself. I will enter into what God has for me!

TODAY'S SCRIPTURE READING:
Ephesians 2

Day Thirteen

The Son of Rahab

Salmon was the father of Boaz (whose mother was Rahab). *Boaz was the father of Obed* (whose mother was Ruth). *Obed was the father of Jesse* (Matthew 1:5 NLT).

Today, let's finally dive into the life of the ancestress of Jesus—Rahab, a Canaanite of the city of Jericho. We first meet her in Joshua 2, when Joshua sent two spies from Israel to scout out Jericho. These two men stayed the night at the house of Rahab the prostitute. However, someone reported their presence to the king of Jericho, and the king ordered Rahab to turn over the spies to him. But Rahab, who had hidden the men, claimed that they had already left (see Josh. 2:1–5).

Rahab made an unusual decision. Instead of siding with her own people, she chose to hide the Israeli spies. This strange choice was rooted in a revelation. Rahab told the spies all that she'd heard about the other lands that Israel had conquered, and she said:

> *I know the Lord has given you this land.... We are all afraid of you. Everyone in the land is living in terror.... For the Lord your God is the supreme God of the heavens above and the earth below* (Joshua 2:9,11 NLT).

Rahab sided with Joshua and the children of Israel because of what she had heard. In fact, according to her, everyone had heard the same thing. All of the people of Jericho had heard about how God delivered Israel from Egypt, how Israel then defeated the giant King Og and his kingdom, and how Israel defended itself again Sihon's attack, overthrowing his entire kingdom (see Josh. 2:10). The key words are *we have heard.*

Over and over, God had told the people of Israel that He was giving them the land of Canaan. The first generation refused to believe it, and they wandered in the desert for 40 years. But the second generation decided to believe God's word, and God defeated the Canaanite nations before them. Rahab heard about what God had done, and she chose to believe as well.

Faith comes by hearing and hearing by the word of God (see Rom. 10:17). When faith builds up in a person's heart, eventually that person must make a decision. Rahab made her decision and declared, "I know the Lord has given you this land....For the Lord your God is the supreme God of the heavens above and the earth below" (Josh 2:9,11 NLT). Rahab's declaration and act of faith transformed her life forever. If God could do it for Rahab, I know He can do it for you!

TODAY'S APPLICATION AND PRAYER

On your phone, refrigerator, mirror, or on something you will see every day, write what God is speaking to your heart about your future. If you feel like you haven't heard God say anything about your future yet, that's okay. Instead, you can write: "I am a new creation in Christ Jesus. My future is as bright as God can make it."

After your write what God is telling you about your future, pray this prayer: "Father, thank You for making me a new creation in Christ Jesus. I ask for further insight and revelation about the future You have for me. In Jesus' name, amen."

TODAY'S CONFESSION

I am a new creation in Christ Jesus. Everything God has said about me is coming to pass. If God could do it for Rahab, I know He can do it for me. The same transforming power that worked in Rahab's life is now at work in my life. In Jesus' name, amen.

TODAY'S SCRIPTURE READING:

Joshua 2; 2 Corinthians 5:17; Hebrews 11:31

DAY FOURTEEN

THE HARLOT OF JERICHO

"I know the Lord has given you this land," she told them… (Joshua 2:9 NLT).

Rahab, as a Jerichoan woman, would have worshipped the Canaanite pantheon of gods. But then she heard about the Lord. (In the Bible, the Lord refers to the God of Israel, called Jehovah or Yahweh.) After what she had heard, she decided to place her faith in Jehovah instead. Because of her faith, she protected the Israeli spies from the king of Jericho. After the king's men had left, Rahab made a request of the two Israeli spies.

Now swear to me by the Lord that you will be kind to me and my family since I have helped you. Give me some guarantee that when Jericho is conquered, you will let me live, along with my father and mother, my brothers and sisters, and all their families (Joshua 2:12–13 NLT).

The spies agreed to save her and her family if she did not betray them and if she followed their exact instructions. When the army of Israel attacked, Rahab should leave the scarlet rope (which they used to escape from her house) hanging from her window. And she must gather all of her family members inside her house (see Josh. 2:14–21).

The rope that had aided the escape of the spies became the symbol of Rahab's protection. The scarlet rope of the prostitute Rahab foreshadowed what the blood of Jesus would do for us. Jericho was soon to be destroyed. All of Jericho had heard the same report that Rahab heard, but she was the only who decided to believe what she heard and act in faith. She chose faith, but the rest of Jericho hardened their hearts in fear. When you chose to believe God's word, God provides a way of escape, just like He did for the spies—and for Rahab. Like Rahab, your faith enables your protection and escape from the destruction of the world. Your faith in what God says will take you from your past into your future.

God "has delivered us from the power of darkness and conveyed us into the kingdom of the Son of His love, in whom we have redemption through His blood, the forgiveness of sins" (Col. 1:13–14). God rescued the spies from the king of Jericho, He saved Rahab and her family from the judgment of Jericho, and He has delivered you from the kingdom of darkness. Now you are part of the Kingdom of God. Rahab's faith also secured her future in a new kingdom among the Israelites (see Josh. 6:25). But the result of Rahab's faith did not end there, as we will see throughout the rest of this book.

Rahab's good tidings of Christmas cheer are this: Your faith can completely disconnect you from the horrors of your past. Your past is not strong enough to rule your future. You are now redeemed. Like Rahab, your faith freed you from your past and placed you in a new Kingdom with a King who has planned a gloriously bright future for you. Putting faith in His plan will enable you to see His wondrous results—just like Rahab.

Today's Application and Prayer

In a notebook or journal, honestly answer the following question:

1. What does it mean to you that Jesus rescued you from your past?

As you answer this question, pray this prayer: "Father, thank You for rescuing me from my past. You have redeemed me, and I am grateful. Show me what limitations I have placed on myself, and help me to break loose of them so that I can walk fully into the expansive future You have for me. In Jesus' name, amen."

Today's Faith Confession

The blood of Jesus has washed away my sins and freed me from the limitations of my past. My past is not strong enough to determine my future because Jesus has redeemed me!

Today's Scripture Reading:

1 Peter 1:18–22; Hebrews 9:12–14; Galatians 3:13–14

DAY FIFTEEN

SCARLET THREAD AND CHRISTMAS DECORATIONS

By faith the harlot Rahab did not perish with those who did not believe, when she had received the spies with peace (Hebrews 11:31).

By now, Christmas decorations are everywhere, and I love it. Trees, garlands, lights, ribbons, and bows fill private and public spaces. Rahab's story has a decoration too—the scarlet rope hanging from her window. Her neighbors probably thought it strange, but I doubt she cared. Rahab kept the rope there in faith, believing she would be delivered from the coming destruction. The walls of Jericho fell supernaturally as the Israelites shouted, but Rahab's house, which was built into one of the walls, remained intact. Faith requires action. Rahab showed her faith by hiding the spies and keeping the scarlet rope in her window. Your faith that God has handled your past and provided a wonderful future for you also requires action. Faith prepares for what it expects to receive.

Imagine you want a large piece of furniture for your house, and someone you trust tells you he is giving you that piece of furniture for Christmas. How would you respond? Would you prepare your house to receive the gift? Faith in that gift would require action. You may need to make space by throwing out junk or reorganizing your existing furniture. You may need to clean the area where you want to place the furniture. You may even need to shift your schedule so you are home when it is delivered. What's certain is, if you believed the gift was coming, you would prepare.

God has prepared a wonderful future for you. Now, you need to prepare to receive it. Analyze your life with the wisdom and insight of the Spirit of God, and then make plans to move forward. A new year is just around the corner. Enter it with clarity, confidence, and conviction that your future is bright.

TODAY'S APPLICATION AND PRAYER

In a notebook or journal, honestly answer the following questions:

1. Do you need to replace any bad habits from your past with habits that will lead you to your future? What are those habits? What habits will you replace them with?

2. Moving successfully into your future will take accountability. Identify an accountability plan or system to help you thrive in your future. (Accountability can happen in community groups or volunteer teams at your local church.)

3. What does your future look like? It is hard to go forward if you don't know where you are going. You don't have to know all the details, but write what you do know.

4. What do you need to do to prepare for your future? What steps do you need to take? Write them down.

5. What will you do when you feel discouraged about your future? Have a plan ready so you can overcome future discouragement.

6. When will you evaluate your progress? It is easy to get off track. Schedule a time every few weeks to evaluate and make sure you are making progress in the right direction. If you notice you are not progressing in a certain area, tweak your plan and then reevaluate in a few weeks.

As you answer these questions, know that I am praying for you. God will give you wisdom, clarity, and understanding, and He will guide your steps. Now pray this prayer: "Father, please give me the Spirit of wisdom and revelation in the knowledge of You. Flood the eyes of my understanding with light so that I may know the hope of Your calling. Thank You for showing me exactly what to do. In Jesus' name, amen."

TODAY'S FAITH CONFESSION

My steps are ordered by the Lord. He delights in every detail of my life. He is leading me and guiding me into all truth, including the truth of my future.

TODAY'S SCRIPTURE READING:

James 2; Ephesians 1:16–21; Psalm 37:22

DAY SIXTEEN

PROVISION FOR YOUR FUTURE

So Joshua spared Rahab the prostitute and her relatives who were with her in the house, because she had hidden the spies Joshua sent to Jericho. And she lives among the Israelites to this day (Joshua 6:25 NLT).

Placing her faith in God completely transformed Rahab's life and positioned her for a marvelous future. Rahab and her family settled in the promised land with the rest of the people of Israel. Rahab eventually married a man named Salmon, and they had a son named Boaz. We first read about the son of Rahab in the Book of Ruth. "Now there was a wealthy and influential man in Bethlehem named Boaz, who was a relative of Naomi's husband, Elimelech" (Ruth 2:1 NLT).

Salmon and Rahab were among the first generation to settle in the promised land; Boaz was part of the second generation. Ruth 2:1 tells us that Boaz was a very wealthy and influential man. In fact, the KJV calls him a "mighty man of wealth." Many people think their future is limited and, at best, average because of the mistakes of their past. However, God wonderfully provided for Rahab, Salmon, and their son Boaz. He did not hold Rahab's past against her. In the Book of Ruth, we see that Boaz was a man of character, wealth, influence, and wisdom. His wealth and influence endured and thrived in the face of a famine and Moabite oppression. Rahab's faith enabled her to have a family that was even able to provide for others in Bethlehem. Her family and her future were not limited. They overflowed with the provision and goodness of God.

The decisions you make to trust God today will set up generational blessings for your children and grandchildren. Leaving your old way of living may seem to put you at a disadvantage and even set you back relationally, financially, career wise, and in other areas. But whatever you give up to follow God, God will replace and give back to you even more. As Abraham realized in Genesis 22, God is Jehovah Jireh. He is the God who sees and provides. As you move into your future, know that you have a benefactor and provider. You have a care-taker, and He will take care of you in grand style.

If God could provide wonderfully for the family of Rahab, He can do the same for you. Faith in God unshackles your future and positions you to experience the best of life. God gave Rahab a family, a future, and a legacy. Imagine what He can do for you! God will provide for you, teach you how to make wise financial decisions, and lead you down the right path in every area of your life.

TODAY'S APPLICATION AND PRAYER

In a notebook or journal, honestly answer the following questions:

1. What has been a generational limit on you and your family?

2. How has this limitation effected your thinking and your expectation for your future?

3. What generational blessing and legacy do you want to leave for those who come after you?

As you answer these questions, pray this prayer: "Father, thank You for being my provider! Please grant me wisdom and understanding concerning my financial affairs. Help me to think beyond the limitations of my family's past. Help me to make decisions that not only revolutionize my life, but also help me to set up a legacy of blessing for those who come after me. In Jesus' name, amen."

TODAY'S CONFESSION

My God will always provide for me. He is Jehovah Jireh. I cast every care upon Him. He takes care of me in grand style. I will not worry about my financial future. I will make financial decisions by the wisdom of God. God is my Shepherd, so I will not lack. My present and my future are filled with His wisdom and provision. The same God who prospered Boaz is prospering me.

TODAY'S SCRIPTURE READING:
Ruth 1–2

THE SON OF RUTH

The two sons married Moabite women. One married a woman named Orpah, and the other a woman named Ruth... (**Ruth 1:4 NLT**).

Ruth was a Moabitess. Although Moab was a descendant of Lot (Abraham's nephew), his descendants became enemies of Israel. They worshipped false gods and tried to hire Balaam to curse Israel. Moab eventually invaded Israeli territory and oppressively ruled over portions of the promised land for 18 years. During that period of oppression, the family of Elimelech moved to Moab, and one of his sons married Ruth.

When Naomi and Ruth moved to Bethlehem, everyone knew Ruth was a Moabitess. But she found favor because of her kindness to Naomi. In Ruth 4, the women said Ruth was better to Naomi than ten sons could have been. Boaz, the son of Rahab, originally showed Ruth favor because of her great kindness to Naomi. He also spoke this blessing over her, "May the Lord, the God of Israel, under whose wings you have come to take refuge, reward you fully for what you have done" (Ruth 2:12 NLT).

When Ruth declared that the God of Israel would be her God, she took God as her refuge. As you journey into your future, you may at times feel apprehensive about what awaits you. As you approach Christmas and the new year, know that God will be your refuge as well. Psalm 91:1–2 says:

> *Those who live in the shelter of the Most High will find rest in the shadow of the Almighty. This I declare about the Lord: He alone is my refuge, my place of safety; he is my God, and I trust him* (NLT).

Declaring that God is your refuge will help you overcome any apprehension and remind you that God is your protector and mighty fortress. He protected

Ruth; He will protect you too! He provided for Rahab; He will provide for you too! Ruth demonstrated several important qualities that will help you move into your future. Ruth was a woman of great kindness, she was an extremely diligent worker, and she took God as her refuge. Great kindness, diligence, and trust in God are essential to stepping into your future.

The Book of Ruth ends with the marriage of Ruth and Boaz. The people of Bethlehem spoke a powerful blessing over their union:

> *May the Lord make this woman who is coming into your home like Rachel and Leah, from whom all the nation of Israel descended...* (Ruth 4:11).

Rachel and Leah were the matriarchs of Israel—yet the people spoke this blessing over a Moabitess. Her past, her former country, became irrelevant. She was now a recipient of blessing. And Ruth did become like Rachel and Leah. Her son Obed, had a son named Jesse, who had a son we call King David. Faith in God took Rahab and Ruth from their former lives and placed them in the lineage of great kings. Faith won't just get you out of something; it will also get you into something! Faith has taken you from your past and placed you in a glorious new future.

Today's Application and Prayer

In a notebook or journal, honestly answer the following questions:

1. Who can you show great kindness to today?

2. How can you make showing kindness part of your lifestyle?

3. What areas of your life can you become more diligent in?

4. What about your future do you feel apprehensive about? How does the revelation that God is your refuge impact that?

As you answer these questions, pray this prayer: "Father, thank You for showing me kindness. Because You live in me, Your kindness lives in me. Help me extend Your kindness to others today. Show me the areas I can become more diligent in. Help me to overcome apprehension, worry, and fear about my future. In Jesus' name, amen."

Today's Confession:

The Lord is my refuge, my salvation, my fortress, and my strength. I will not be afraid of my future because I know God is my refuge. God is making a way for me. God has been extremely kind to me, and He is enabling me to extend that kindness to others. My future is filled with the kindness and goodness of God.

Today's Scripture Reading:

Psalm 91

DAY EIGHTEEN

THE SON OF DAVID

Salmon was the father of Boaz. Boaz was the father of Obed. Obed was the father of Jesse. Jesse was the father of David (Ruth 4:21–22 NLT).

David, one of the most famous kings in the Bible, is a prominent ancestor of Jesus. He is so prominent that the New Testament begins, "This is a record of the ancestors of Jesus the Messiah, a descendant of David and of Abraham" (Matthew 1:1 NLT). Jesus even adopted the Messianic title, "Son of David." On the night of His birth, the angels told the shepherds in the field, "For there is born to you this day in the city of David a Savior, who is Christ the Lord" (Luke 2:11). God even promised David that one of his descendants would sit on his throne forever (see 2 Sam. 7).

But David did not start as the famous and beloved king. He started as a shepherd who was looked down on by his family. His father even left him in the field when the prophet Samuel came to visit. Samuel was the leading prophet in Israel and one of the last judges. God had used him mightily since he was a child. Samuel's visit to Bethlehem drew a lot of attention. The fact that he came in peace and invited Jesse and his sons to the sacrifice was a high honor.

As Samuel met Jesse's eldest son, Samuel initially thought he must be the anointed one the Lord sent him to look for. Yet God told Samuel that he was not the one, that He was not looking at their outward appearance, but at their hearts (see 1 Sam. 16:6–10). Samuel met all of the sons in the house and realized that the Lord had not chosen any of them. So Samuel asked if there were any other sons, and Jesse called for the youngest—David, who was with the sheep. When David appeared, the Lord told Samuel, "Arise, anoint him; for this is the one!" and the Spirit of the Lord came upon David (see 1 Sam. 16:12–13).

David was left out, but God still saw Him. God was looking at hearts (not appearance), and in David's heart He found what He was looking for. He called him

"David the son of Jesse, a man after My own heart, who will do all My will" (Acts 13:22). Young David had a vitally important quality that will help you experience the future God has for you—complete and total commitment to the plan of God. If you are determined to do what God has called you to do, you will experience promotion like David did.

God anointed David in front of his brothers, his father, and the elders of Bethlehem (see 2 Sam. 16:13). The anointing is God's power and ability. When Samuel anointed David, David received empowerment to do what God called him to do. In moments, David went from being the overlooked shepherd to being the anointed future king. Do not let the opinions of others keep you from fulfilling the plan of God for your life. They may not offer you a seat at the table, but God knows how to get you where you need to be. In the same way that He anointed and empowered David, He will anoint and empower you to fulfill His plan.

TODAY'S APPLICATION AND PRAYER

In a notebook or journal, honestly answer the following questions:

1. When have you felt left out or forgotten?

2. Has being left out or forgotten impacted how you see yourself?

3. Has that feeling become a driving force in your life? Are you trying to compensate for that feeling in some way?

As you answer these questions, pray this prayer: "Father, I forgive those who have forgotten about me. I forgive those who made me feel left out. Help me to overcome these feelings and negative motivations. Thank You for always seeing me and for anointing me. Help me to always remember that Your opinion matters more than any other. In Jesus' name, amen."

Today's Confession

I am anointed. God has anointed and empowered me to fulfill His plan for my life. I will not allow the opinions of others to talk me out of God's plan for my life. I will do all the things God has called me to do because He has anointed me.

Today's Scripture Reading:
2 Samuel 7

DAY NINETEEN

THE SON OF BATHSHEBA

And Jesse begot David the king. David the king begot Solomon by her who had been the wife of Uriah (Matthew 1:6).

David—the great, prominent, anointed, giant-slaying, psalm-writing king of Israel—made a horrific decision. This decision destroyed a family, brought destruction to David's family, and caused future family drama and trauma for the household of David. When summarizing David's life and reign, 1 Kings 15:5 says, "David did what was right in the eyes of the Lord, and had not turned aside from anything that He commanded him all the days of his life, except in the matter of Uriah the Hittite."

Uriah the Hittite was one of thirty elite warriors known as David's Mighty Men (see 2 Sam. 23). He was a man of integrity and was dedicated to the cause of Israel. But David murdered Uriah, in a horrific abuse of power, in order to take Uriah's wife, Bathsheba. As a result, many other Israeli soldiers also died, and David opened the door to Absalom's future rebellion and further death and destruction for David's family. David suffered greatly for this decision; he should have been cancelled, but God forgave him. David and Bathsheba married and had a son named Solomon.

Although Solomon was the son of a king, he was born into a situation created by a murderous abuse of power. The son of Bathsheba could have carried a stigma with him because of his father's actions. Some would have thought this child could never be king because of the circumstances surrounding his birth. But Solomon was the one God chose to be king. In fact, God had a special name for him; God called him Jedidiah, which means beloved of the Lord. God loved the son of Bathsheba, and he became the wisest and richest king on earth.

Maybe your problem is not letting go of your past, but letting go of the situation you were born into and the circumstances of your upbringing. Perhaps you still face challenges and problems related to your upbringing. It is not your fault, but it is your fight. You are not to blame for the mistakes of your parents. You are not to blame for what they didn't teach you or give you as a child. It's not your fault, but it is your fight. You must move past and let go of the limiting circumstances of your upbringing to move into the future God has for you.

If God could raise Solomon to become the richest and wisest king of his era, He can do wonderful things for you and through you. God is looking at you with love just like He looked at Solomon. You are greatly loved by Him. God wants to completely transform your life and enable you to give your kids, grandkids, and beyond a far grander start than you had. Your birth does not determine your future; now you are born again.

TODAY'S APPLICATION AND PRAYER

In a notebook or journal, honestly answer the following questions and pray these prayers:

1. Are you carrying any embarrassment or shame related to what your parents or any members of your family have done? If so, pray this prayer: "Father, I release the embarrassment and shame. I thank You that the mistakes of my family do not determine Your love for me or the future that You have for me. In Jesus' name, amen."

2. Have you forgiven that family member for creating this situation? If not, pray: "Father, I forgive that person for placing me and my family in this situation. In Jesus' name, amen."

TODAY'S CONFESSION

My background does not determine my future. The way I was born does not determine my destination or potential for success. I have been born again. The Spirit of God lives on the inside of me. Greater is He who is in me than he who is in the world. My heavenly Father loves me, and He has lovingly orchestrated a wonderful future for me.

TODAY'S SCRIPTURE READING:

Psalm 113

THE SON OF MANASSEH

Hezekiah was the father of Manasseh. Manasseh was the father of Amon. Amon was the father of Josiah (**Matthew 1:10 NLT**).

The Wet Bandits of Home Alone, the Grinch, Mr. Potter of *It's A Wonderful Life* Ebenezer Scrooge (before his conversion)—we are familiar with the infamous villains of classic Christmas movies. And when reading the story of the nativity, we think of the villainous King Herod, but we often overlook another villain connected to the story of Christmas. This villain is another ancestor of Jesus—King Manasseh.

Manasseh was the longest-reigning monarch of the kingdom of Judah. His father Hezekiah did wonderful things and followed God, but Manasseh chose another course. He embraced pagan practices, rebuilt pagan shrines, constructed altars for false gods, sacrificed his son to these idols, practiced sorcery, led the people of Israel away from God, and engaged in all kinds of evil— even placing an idol he had carved in God's temple (see 2 Chron. 33:2–10). Manasseh also "murdered many innocent people until Jerusalem was filled from one end to the other with innocent blood" (2 Kings 21:16 NLT). He was the most wicked king of Judah.

Eventually, the Assyrian army captured Manasseh and imprisoned him in Babylon, but his story does not end there. While in prison, Manasseh finally sought the Lord and humbled himself before Him in repentance. God not only listened to Manasseh's prayer, but He also brought him back to his kingdom in Jerusalem (see 2 Chron. 33:12). Because of God's mighty work on his behalf, "Manasseh finally realized that the Lord alone is God" (2 Chron. 33:13 NLT).

When even the most wicked Judean king turned back to God while in prison, God listened and had mercy on him. For the rest of his days, Manasseh served God and did his best to encourage Judah to do the same. It is never too late to let God turn your story around.

Perhaps you feel like you have been the villain for the majority of your life. You know God has forgiven you, but you don't think you can do much to make up for all the bad. Or perhaps you don't think you have a lot of time left to do good on this planet. If God can forgive, restore, and then work through Manasseh, He can do the same for all of us. The time you have left on this earth is a gift. Whether you have years or decades ahead of you, you can make the most of your time by dedicating yourself to fulfilling God's plan for your life. As you'll see in today's scripture reading, God can and will add years to your life. Your life is not over; God can still make a difference through you! Our Messiah is a son of Manasseh. After all that Manasseh did, God still restored him and chose to place the Messiah among his descendants.

TODAY'S APPLICATION AND PRAYER

In a notebook or journal, honestly answer the following questions:

1. Have you limited the impact of your future due to the mistakes of your past?

2. What are some decisions you can make today to plan to live a long, healthy, and fruitful life? Do you need to make any health or diet changes as well?

As you answer these questions, pray this prayer: "Father, I choose to believe Your Word. In Psalm 91:16, You said You would satisfy me with long life. I choose to believe Your Word. Help me to plan for a long and fruitful life. Show me what I need to do to add years to my life. Help me to make healthy decisions so I can live a long and fruitful life. I ask You to renew my youth. In Jesus' name, amen."

Today's Confession

My life has a purpose. My God is renewing my youth and adding years to my life. My best is ahead of me, and I am taking advantage of every opportunity God brings my way. I am redeeming the time.

Today's Scripture Reading:

Psalm 91:16; 103:1–6; Ephesians 5:15–17; Proverbs 3:1–2, 13–16; 9:10–11; 10:27

DAY TWENTY-ONE

GETTING THE BEST DEAL

So be careful how you live. Don't live like fools, but like those who are wise. Make the most of every opportunity in these evil days. Don't act thoughtlessly, but understand what the Lord wants you to do (**Ephesians 5:15–17 NLT**).

As we approach Christmas Day, last-minute sales and deals are appearing everywhere. Whether they are large online retailers or local stores, businesses are working hard to convince consumers to get their last Christmas purchases from them. Have you taken advantage of a special deal this season? Did you get something on sale instead of paying full price?

The apostle Paul instructed the church of Ephesus to redeem the time by taking advantage of every opportunity. The original language of the scripture paints the picture of someone buying up all of the deals in a marketplace. The same applies to us. God will bring opportunities your way, but you must take advantage of them. You must view the opportunities in your life the same way a keen shopper views the best deals. The ability to take advantage of the opportunities God brings your way will accelerate your move into your future.

In order to take advantage of divine opportunities, you must be prepared. Faith prepares for what it expects to receive. Preparation takes place as you dedicate yourself to God's plan for your life by following the leading of His Spirit, diligently studying what God has called you to do, and faithfully doing what God has put in front of you. Preparation is never lost time.

As you move into your future, God may give you assignments that seem unimportant. Give your all to these assignments anyway. Every assignment from God prepares you for future assignments. Every leading from God and every opportunity He brings your way are steps into the glorious future He has for you. Don't let divine opportunities pass you by; prepare to go into your future today!

TODAY'S APPLICATION AND PRAYER

In a notebook or journal, honestly answer the following questions:

1. In reference to what God has called you to do, in what ways can you be better prepared? What steps can you take right now to enhance your preparation in this area?

2. What assignment do you think little of right now? How can you show yourself even more faithful in this area?

As you answer these questions, pray this prayer: "Father, please show me areas where I can be better prepared. And show me what steps I need to take. Help me to be faithful in the little so that I can be faithful in the much.

TODAY'S CONFESSION

I make the most of every opportunity that God brings my way. I prepare and study to show myself approved. I am faithful and diligent in everything I do. I listen to the voice of the Spirit of God, and I follow His leading. I take advantage of every opportunity that God brings my way.

Today's Scripture Reading:
Matthew 2; Luke 16:10

The Son of Joseph

Now the birth of Jesus the Messiah was as follows: when His mother Mary had been betrothed to Joseph, before they came together she was found to be pregnant by the Holy Spirit. And her husband Joseph, since he was a righteous man and did not want to disgrace her, planned to send her away secretly (**Matthew 1:18–19**).

Joseph, the husband of Mary is an often-unsung hero of the Christmas story. Have you ever wondered what qualities God looked for in the man He would trust to raise the Messiah? Joseph had these qualities, and if we have them, they will help us move into the future God has for us. Matthew 1:18 says that Joseph was a righteous man. Other translations say that he was a good or just man. Joseph was a man of character. He did not understand what was going on with Mary. I'm sure he felt slighted, hurt, betrayed. Despite his deep feelings, because he was a good man, he decided to end things quietly in order to protect Mary. But when the angel appeared to Joseph, Joseph quickly believed and quickly changed his plans to follow the angel's instructions. Joseph followed the directions of God all throughout Matthew 2.

In the same way that Joseph was a man of character, you must be a person of character. Taking advantage of divine opportunities can take you into grand rooms of influence; but character will keep you in those rooms. As the old saying goes, "You cannot fire a cannon from a canoe." If you fire a cannon from a canoe, the canoe sinks. In the same way, if you do not have character to sustain you, opportunities and giftings can sink you.

Every believer in Jesus should develop the character traits of Jesus found in Galatians 5:22–23. We develop these traits as we grow our personal relationship with Jesus through prayer, communion with Him, reading the Word, and applying the Word to our lives. The character traits of Jesus (the fruit of the Spirit) are not behavior modifications; these traits are the result of the Spirit's indwelling presence as He transforms us.

In the same way that Joseph was quick to follow God's leading, you must be quick to follow the leading of the Spirit of God. The Holy Spirit is actively producing the character traits of Jesus within you and leading you into the future God has for you. Earlier in this devotional we discussed the gifts of forgiveness and righteousness. God also gave you another gift—the Holy Spirit. When you made Jesus the Lord of your life, the Holy Spirit moved in on the inside of you to lead you, guide you, help you, and produce the character traits of Jesus in you. The Holy Spirit also empowers you to make a difference in other people's lives when He rests upon you.

You need both operations of the Spirit of God in your life, and they will grow as you faithfully cultivate your relationship with Jesus, your prayer life, and your time in the Word. The Holy Spirit is the one who empowers you to live the future that the heavenly Father has for you.

Today's Application and Prayer

In a notebook or journal, honestly answer the following question:

1. What is the fruit of the Spirit that you need to develop the most?

As you answer this question, pray this prayer: "Father, thank You for the precious gift of the Holy Spirit. Please help me to be sensitive to His leading and voice. Help me to yield to His Word in me so that He can develop the fruit of the Spirit within me. In Jesus' name, amen."

Today's Confession

The Holy Spirit lives big on the inside of me. He is producing in me the character traits of Jesus. Because of His indwelling presence, love, joy, peace, patience, kindness, goodness, faithfulness, gentleness, and self-control are developing on the inside of me. I am a person of character, and I am quick to follow the leading of the Spirit of God.

Today's Scripture Reading:

Luke 1:1–38; Romans 8:14–16; Galatians 5:22–23

THE SON OF MARY

The angel replied, "The Holy Spirit will come upon you, and the power of the Most High will overshadow you. So the baby to be born will be holy, and he will be called the Son of God" (Luke 1:35 NLT).

The Holy Spirit empowers the Christian life; He desires to empower you and work through you to do amazing things. As Gabriel proclaimed to Mary, the miraculous birth of the Messiah was a work of the Holy Spirit's power. Throughout Luke's writings (the Gospel of Luke and the Book of Acts), we see the Holy Spirit's willingness to rest upon people and empower them to do what they could not do on their own. Near the beginning of our advent journey, we saw that Elizabeth acknowledged Mary's faith as the key ingredient to her experience. In the same way that Mary's faith enabled her to become the mother of the Messiah, your faith will connect you to the power of the Holy Spirit.

One of the things I love about this season are the Christmas lights. My favorite are the multi-colored lights; I love how they light up the darkness of the night with their radiant beauty. For all of those beautiful lights to work, they must be plugged into a power source. In the same way, you cannot shine if you're not connected to the power source. God has brought you through too much for you not to shine. The Holy Spirit will enable you to shine. As you yield to His work in you, as you develop the character traits of Jesus, as you bring more people to Jesus, and as you grow in your relationship with Jesus, you shine more and more.

Jesus wants you to shine. He is not ashamed of you or your past. He is not ashamed of your background or your upbringing. He is not ashamed of you. Jesus is not ashamed to call us His brothers and sisters (see Heb. 2:11). Jesus does not want you to hide your light because of your past, your upbringing, your background, or your mistakes. He sent the Holy Spirit to help you be who He's called you to be—light. As Jesus said:

You're here to be light, bringing out the God-colors in the world. God is not a secret to be kept. We're going public with this, as public as a city on a hill. If I make you light-bearers, you don't think I'm going to hide you under a bucket, do you? I'm putting you on a light stand. Now that I've put you there on a hilltop, on a light stand—shine! Keep open house; be generous with your lives. By opening up to others, you'll prompt people to open up with God, this generous Father in heaven (Matthew 5:14 MSG)

Many Christians sing, "This little light of mine, I'm gonna let it shine," but Jesus never called us to have a little light. When I think about the light Jesus wants us to have, I'm reminded of the *Home Improvement* TV show from the '90s. The main character was known for having over the top, elaborate, exceedingly bright Christmas displays. This is the type of light Jesus wants to shine through you. The Holy Spirit is working in you to shine the God-colors to the world. Don't hide your light; be who God has created you to be. God wants you to shine everywhere you go.

Today's Application and Prayer

In a notebook or journal, honestly answer the following question:

1. When you read today's devotional, what was the first place in your local community that you thought of? Your office, gym, coffee shop, or somewhere else? How can you shine brighter in that place?

As you ponder these questions, pray this prayer: "Lord, thank You for calling me to be light. I believe, with the empowerment of the Holy Spirit, I can shine brighter. Please grant me wisdom and insight on how to shine brighter in this area. In Jesus' name, amen."

Today's Confession

I am the light of the world. The light of the glorious gospel is shining in me and through me. I yield to the working of the Holy Spirit every single day of my life. As a result, I am shining brighter and brighter.

Today's Scripture Reading

Luke 1:39–80; Proverbs 4:18

DAY TWENTY-FOUR

IT'S CELEBRATION TIME!

For whatever things were written before were written for our learning, that we through the patience and comfort of the Scriptures might have hope.... Now may the God of hope fill you with all joy and peace in believing, that you may abound in hope by the power of the Holy Spirit (**Romans 15:4, 13**).

Merry Christmas! As you finish your preparations on this Christmas Eve and proceed into the celebrations of Christmas Day, I want to wish you the merriest of Christmases. This wish of mine is akin to the wish of 3 John 2 that you would prosper in all things. It is a fervent desire and prayer. Over the last 24 days, we have journeyed together—exploring the lineage of Jesus and the gifts of forgiveness, righteousness, and the Holy Spirit. In just one week, we will be looking into the dawning of a brand-new year. You are ready for the new year. You are ready for your future!

The stories of the lineage of Jesus are instructional, but they are also designed to give us hope. Biblical hope is positive expectation based on our knowledge of the faithfulness of God and the truth of the Word of God. Hope always deals with the future. When we talk about our dreams for the future, we border on the biblical realm of hope. As the God of hope, God wants us to overflow with hope through the power of the Holy Spirit in our lives.

He wants you to have hope for you future, hope for your life, hope for your family, hope for your relationships, hope for your health, hope for your finances, hope for your career, and hope for every area of your life. If your hope is based on the Word of God and the leading of His Spirit, you will have miraculous results just like Abraham. Your faith in God and His plan will radically transform your life just like faith changed the lives of Rahab and Ruth. Whether you identify most with Abraham, Rahab, Ruth, David, Bathsheba, Solomon, Manasseh, Joseph, or Mary, God has a wonderful future for you that you are now ready to take another step toward. Jesus, the son of Rahab, loves you. Your future is waiting for you. Christmas is a celebration of Christ and His anointing. You have so many reasons to celebrate what Jesus and His anointing has done for you. Enjoy your celebration. Merry Christmas!

TODAY'S APPLICATION AND PRAYER

In a notebook or journal, honestly answer the following questions:

1. How will you celebrate the progress you made while reading this devotional?

2. How will you daily remind yourself of the truths that you have learned in this devotional?

As you answer these questions pray this prayer of thanksgiving: "Lord, thank You for everything You have done for me. Thank You for Jesus. Thank You for sending the Holy Spirit to live within me and rest upon me.

Thank You for forgiving me. Thank You for the gift of righteousness. Thank You for designing a good plan for my life. Thank You for what You have spoken to me through this devotional. Help me live these truths as I go forward into the glorious future You have for me. In Jesus' name, amen."

TODAY'S CONFESSION

My God is filling me with all joy and peace in believing. I am overflowing with hope. I choose to be joyful in anticipation of my future. I will keep celebrating what God has done for me. This will be my most joyful Christmas yet. My future is bright. This coming year will be my best one so far. I will operate by the wisdom of God. I will live in the favor of God. I will flow with the anointing of God. I will yield to the direction of the Spirit of God, and He will show me what to do all year long. I have entered into the greatest days of my life so far. My days will continually grow brighter and will overflow with the goodness of God.

TODAY'S SCRIPTURE READING:
Luke 2; 3 John

ABOUT KERRICK BUTLER II

Kerrick A. R. Butler II serves as Senior Pastor of Faith Christian Center headquartered in Austell, Georgia, with satellite campuses throughout the metro Atlanta area. He is a graduate of Word of Faith Bible Training Center and Oral Roberts University. Kerrick believes wholeheartedly in sharing the message of Jesus through creative avenues to help readers apply Bible truths to their everyday lives. Kerrick, his wife, Racquel, and their beautiful family reside in Atlanta.

FAITH+

Search "**FAITH+**" in your preferred app store or scan the QR Code below.

Download the **FAITH+** app to stream messages from Pastor Kerrick, special content for this book, and thousands of hours of content to help you add to your faith!

From
KERRICK BUTLER

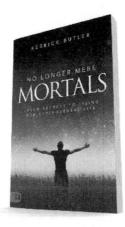

Real-Life Superheroes

YOU are Gods supernatural solution for a world beset with giant problems.

Pastor Kerrick Butler II encourages us that the problems we face in the world today must be addressed by a church who understands that we are not merely mortal, but supernaturally empowered by the Holy Spirit to conquer the Goliaths of our day.

In *No Longer Mere Mortals*, Kerrick shares how to

- Operate in Gods power as a lifestyle not a rare, momentary encounter
- Be empowered as a super human not just as an apostle, prophet, evangelist, pastor, or teacher
- Grow by leaps and bounds in daily Christian disciplines
- Understand who you are in Christ and what God has already accomplished in your life
- Unleash the supernatural powers God has already given you over specific issues

Defeat the Goliaths staring you down. You may not wear a cape, but God made you superhuman just the same!

Purchase your copy wherever books are sold

Equipping Believers to Walk in the Abundant Life
John 10:10b

Connect with us on

Facebook @ HarrisonHousePublishers

and Instagram @ HarrisonHousePublishing

so you can stay up to date with news

about our books and our authors.

Visit us at **www.harrisonhouse.com**

Made in United States
Troutdale, OR
11/13/2023

14538155R00064